I Marry You Because…

by Peter McWilliams

Cover design by Paul LeBus
Interior design by Victoria Marine

Published by Prelude Press
8165 Mannix Drive
Los Angeles, California 90046
213-650-9571

Other books by Peter McWilliams:

POETRY

Come Love with Me and Be My Life
For Lovers and No Others
The Hard Stuff: Love
Love: An Experience Of
Love Is Yes
Come To My Senses
Catch Me with Your Smile

PERSONAL GROWTH

How to Survive The Loss of a Love
(with Melba Colgrove, Ph.D.
and Harold Bloomfield, M.D.

You Can't Afford the Luxury
of a Negative Thought
(with John-Roger)

COMPUTERS

The Personal Computer Book

Published by and available from
Prelude Press
8165 Mannix Drive
Los Angeles, California 90046
213-650-9571

I Marry You Because…

*What do I
get from
loving you?
Loving.
You.*

JOHN-ROGER

I marry you
because
you
are the nicest
thing I could
ever do for
myself.

*I would like to have
engraved inside every
wedding band
"Be kind to one another."
This is the Golden Rule
of marriage and the secret
of making love last
through the years.*

RANDOLPH RAY

_____

I marry you
because
"we"
is better than
"me."

_____

We never live so intensely as when we love strongly. We never realize ourselves so vividly as when we are in full glow of love for others.

WALTER RAUSCHENBUSCH

I marry you
because
we are such
good friends
you & I.
After being
with you
for only
a little while,
I no longer
relate to
sadness.

*Love is a portion of
the soul itself,
and it is of the same nature
as the celestial breathing of
the atmosphere of paradise.*

VICTOR HUGO

I marry you
because
together we discover
the secret spaces of the gods.

Marriage is a fan club
with only two fans.

ADRIAN HENRI

I marry you
because
everything
reminds me
of you.

*Love is the greatest
educational institution
on earth.*

CHANNING POLLOCK

I marry you
because
of what I know
and what
I want to
find out.

Lyndon was the most outspoken, straightforward, determined person I'd ever encountered. I knew I'd met something remarkable — but I didn't know quite what.

LADY BIRD JOHNSON

I marry you
because
I enjoy you.

*When one has once fully
entered the realm of love,
the world
— no matter how imperfect —
becomes rich and beautiful,
it consists solely of
opportunities for love.*

SOREN KIERKEGAARD

I marry you
because
in holding you
I am held.

*A marriage between mature
people is not an escape but a
commitment shared by two
people that becomes part of
their commitment to
themselves and society.*

BETTY FRIEDAN

I marry you
because
you are now a part of my life.
In all decisions
you are a consideration.
In all problems
(mostly in terms of solution)
you are a factor.
In all joy you
are sharing;
in all sorrow
support.

My most brilliant achievement was my ability to persuade my wife to marry me.

WINSTON CHURCHILL

I marry you
because
familiarity
breeds
consent.

The love we have in our youth is superficial compared to the love that an old man has for his old wife.

WILL DURANT

I marry you
because
in those rare
moments when
all desires
have been fulfilled,
my mind
rests
on only
you.

Love does not consist in gazing at each other but in looking outward together in the same direction.

ANTOINE DE SAINT-EXUPERY

When two people love each other, they don't look at each other, they look in the same direction.

GINGER ROGERS

I marry you
because
we can grow,
not together,
but very
nearby.

*Love is the true means
by which the world is
enjoyed.*

THOMAS TRAHERNE

I marry you
because
the love
I give you
is second hand:

I feel it first.

There is no more lovely,
friendly and charming
relationship, communion or
company than a
good marriage.

MARTIN LUTHER

1569

I marry you
because,
although
God
created
all things,
He took
special care
in crafting
the rose
and you.

*A successful marriage
requires falling in love
many times, always with
the same person.*

MIGNON MCLAUGHLIN

I marry you
because
when you smile,
I forget where I am,
and it takes me
longer each time
to remember again.

*In love, all of life's
contradictions dissolve and
disappear. Only in love are
unity and duality
not in conflict.*

RABINDRANATH TAGORE

I marry you
because
our
union
is a
reunion
with creation.

Love is friendship set on fire.

JEREMY TAYLOR

I marry you
because
everyone sighs at
sunsets and roses.

I sigh at
sunsets and roses
and you.

Love is a taste of paradise.

SHOLOM ALEICHEM

I marry you
because
no one
makes me happier
than you.

*Love is the heart's
immortal thirst to be
completely known and
all forgiven.*

HENRY VAN DYKE

I marry you
because
no one
makes you happier
than me.

Love is the fusion
of two hearts
— the union of two lives —
the coming together
of two tributaries.

PETER MARSHALL

I marry you
because
in you
I am
complete.

*Marriage is three parts love
and seven parts forgiveness.*

LANGDON MITCHELL

I marry you
because
what we have
joined together,
let no one
put us under.

*Brigham Young is
the most married man
I ever saw in my life.*

CHARLES FARRAR BROWNE

I marry you
because
marrying is
saying
"I do"
and God saying
"Yes, you do!"

Charles is life itself
— pure life force,
like sunlight —
and it is for this that I
married him and this is
what holds me to him —
caring always,
caring desperately what
happens to him and
whatever he happens
to be involved in.

ANNE MORROW LINDBERGH

I marry you
because
I need to be
cared for;
but,
more importantly,
I need to
care.

*To love is to
admire with the heart;
to admire is to
love with the mind.*

THEOPHILE GAUTIER

I marry you
because
when I hear
the phrase
"dearly beloved"
I think only
of you.

A coward is incapable
of exhibiting love;
it is the prerogative
of the brave.

MAHATMA GANDHI

I marry you
because
we believe
in meeting
life's challenges
heart-on.

*Love gives us in a moment
what we can hardly attain
by effort after years of toil.*

GOETHE

I marry you
because
I want to
celebrate
us.

A lady of 47 who
has been married 27 years
and has 6 children
knows what love really is
and once described it
for me like this:
"Love is what you've been
through with somebody."

JAMES THURBER

I marry you
because
when
something wonderful
happens,
I can't wait
to share it
with you.

*It is a lovely thing to have
a husband and wife
developing together.
That is what marriage really
means; helping one another
to reach the full status
of being persons,
responsible and
autonomous beings who
do not run away from life.*

PAUL TOURNIER

I marry you
because
I believe
I can learn
devotion
faster than
I learned
long division.

Among those whom I like,
I can find
no common denominator,
but among those
whom I love,
I can;
all of them make me laugh.

W.H. AUDEN

I marry you
because
you make
me laugh.

LUCY: *We have had fun,*
haven't we honey?
RICKY: *Yes sir. These fifteen years have*
been the best years of my life.
What's the matter?
LUCY: *We've only been married*
thirteen years.
RICKY: *Oh. Well... I mean it*
seems like fifteen.
LUCY: *What!?*
RICKY: *No... uh... uh... uh...*
what I mean is,
it doesn't... uh... seem possible...
that all that fun could have been
crammed into only thirteen years.
LUCY: *Well, you certainly*
wormed out of that one.

I marry you
because
I can make
you laugh.

I am most
immoderately married:
The Lord God has taken
my heaviness away;
I have merged, like the bird,
with the bright air,
And my thought flies to the
place by the bo-tree.
Being, not doing,
is my first joy.

THEODORE ROETHKE

I marry you
because
marriage is
a state
not to be
entered into
heavily.

The sum which two married
people owe to one another
defies calculation.
It is an infinite debt,
which can only be discharged
through all eternity.

GOETHE

I marry you
because
I care about
caring for
you.

*A wise lover values
not so much
the gift of the lover
as the love of the giver.*

THOMAS KEMPIS

I marry you
because
you give me
the gift of
receiving.

To repress a harsh answer,
to confess a fault,
and to stop (right or wrong)
in the midst of self-defense,
in gentle submission,
sometimes requires
a struggle like life and death;
but these three efforts
are the golden threads
with which
domestic happiness is woven.

CAROLINE GILMAN
(1794-1888)

I marry you
because
you teach
me things
I never thought
I knew.

*Love is not a union
merely between
two creatures —
it is a union between
two spirits.*

FREDERICK W. ROBERTSON

I marry you
because
when I hear
the phrase
"sacred union"
I do not
think of the
Teamsters.

There is only
one terminal dignity —
love.
And the story of a love
is not important —
what is important
is that one is capable of love.
It is perhaps the only glimpse
we are permitted of eternity.

HELEN HAYS

I marry you
because,
considering you,
what else
could I do?

*To love someone is to see
a miracle invisible to others.*

FRANCOIS MAURIAC

I marry you
because
you are my
miracle.

To love is to choose.

JOSEPH ROUX

I marry you
because
commitment
is something
one grows into
and then
grows from.

You will reciprocally promise love,
loyalty and matrimonial honesty.
We only want for you this day
that these words constitute
the principle of your entire life;
and that with the help
of the divine grace
you will observe these solemn vows
that today, before God,
you formulate.

POPE JOHN PAUL II

I marry you
because
God loves
our love.

Two such as you with
such a master speed

Cannot be parted
nor be swept away

From one another
once you are agreed

That life is only
life forevermore

Together
wing to wing
and oar to oar.

ROBERT FROST

I marry you
because
we rhyme.

*Love is the only sane
and satisfactory answer
to the problem
of human existence.*

ERICH FROMM

I marry you
because,
no matter
what the
question,
we are
each other's
answer.

Love is an act of
endless forgiveness,
a tender look
which becomes a habit.

PETER USTINOV

I marry you
because
you're
The One.

I marry you
because
I love you.